# Communication in the U.S.A.
# THEN & NOW

**Maya Franklin**

# Table of Contents

| | |
|---|---|
| Hi, Grandma! | 3 |
| Let's Talk | 6 |
| Mail *Then* | 8 |
| Mail *Now* | 12 |
| News *Then* | 16 |
| News *Now* | 18 |
| A Whole New Communication | 20 |
| Communication Time Line | 22 |
| Glossary | 24 |

# Hi, Grandma!

"Mom, I want to tell Grandma about my new bike," you say.

She answers, "That's a good idea. Would you like to call or write to her? You can send a letter or an e-mail message. You can call her on her cell phone or send her a fax. You can also tell Grandma in person when we fly to her house for a visit. What would you like to do?"

"Wow! I have a lot of choices, don't I?" you respond.

**Communication** is the way we tell each other things. We can do it with our voices or through writing and reading. We can do it with our eyes and movements. That is called body language. Some people even do it with their hands. That is called sign language.

You really do have many **communication** choices. But, if you were born in the United States in colonial times, you would not have had so many choices.

So, how would you talk to your grandmother?

If she lived in your town, you could visit her. If she lived far away, you could write a letter, or you could visit her by walking, riding a horse, or taking a boat.

And that is it. There were no more choices.

# Let's Talk

People mainly communicate by talking. But talking today is not the same as it was then. For example, many of the words are different. The chart on page 7 will show you some differences.

Some people say that people then had better **vocabularies** than people do now. We know they spoke in more formal ways. People today often use slang, and they speak more simply.

> **Vocabularies** are the words people know without using the dictionary. **Slang** words are words people make up or use in new ways. Slang is usually not used in writing. The word "cool" instead of "good" is an example of slang. Do you know any other examples?

Here are a few words that have changed from then to now.

| Then | Now |
|---|---|
| pompion | pumpkin |
| pottage | salad |
| vergi | vinegar |
| forced eggs | scrambled eggs |
| whortleberries | blueberries |
| pipkins | pans |
| trencher | plate |
| sallats | spinach |
| breeches | pants |
| jerkin | vest |
| cassock | cape |
| petticoat | skirt |
| slip time | house slippers |

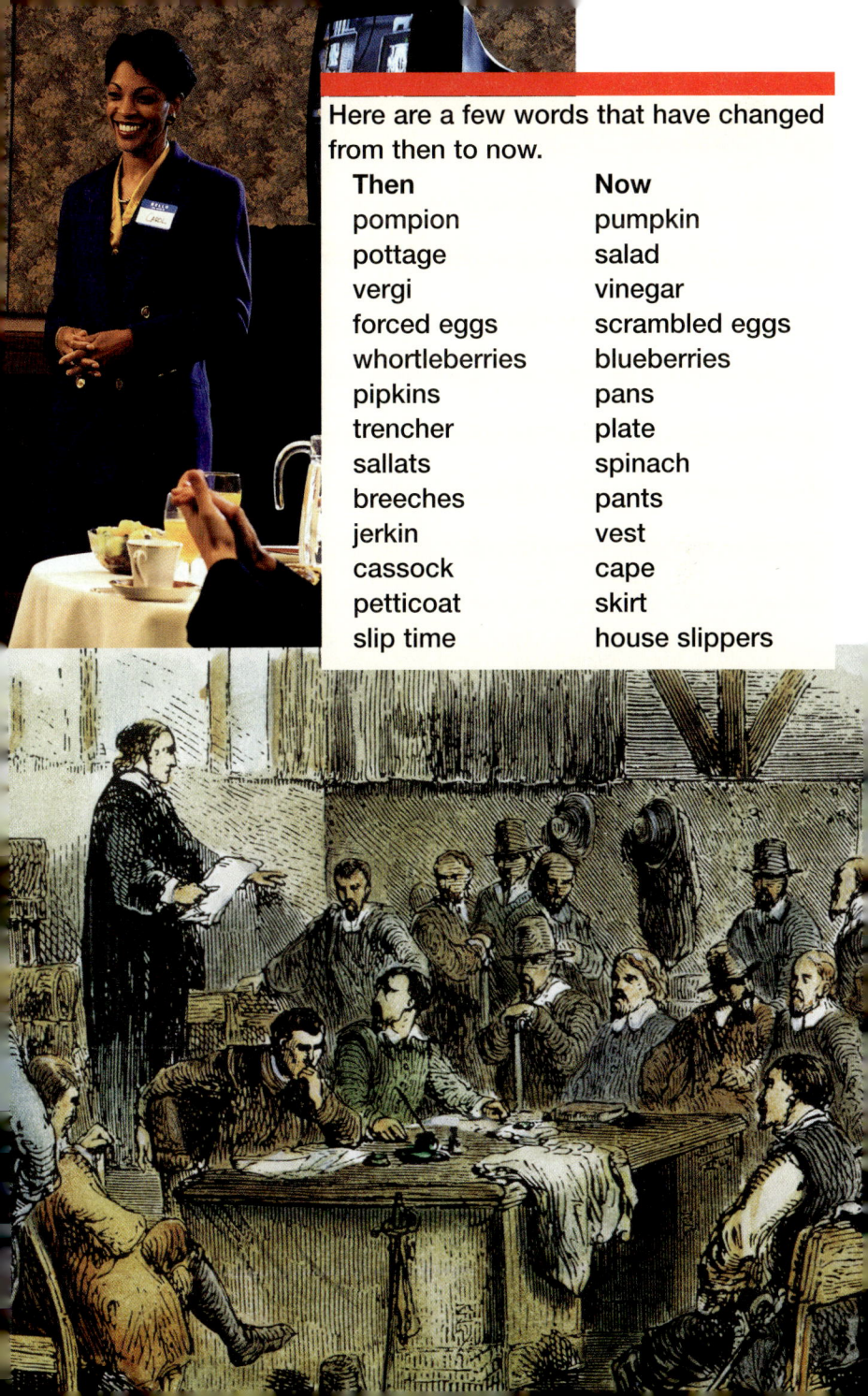

# Mail *Then*

Today we have mail service. People then did, too, but it was different.

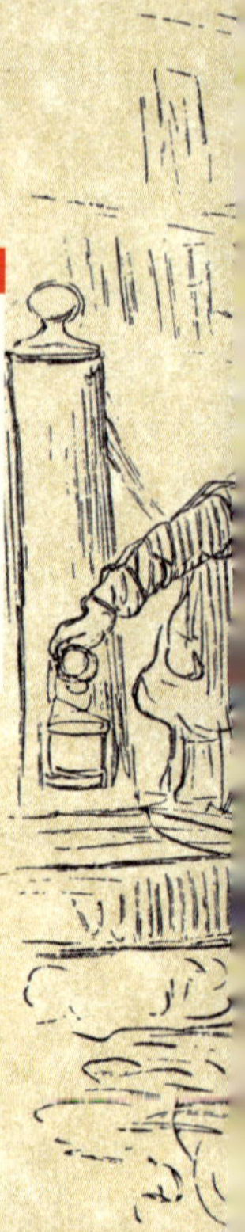

**How Often?**

People who lived in small towns far away from main cities were lucky to send or receive mail once each month.

People then had no post offices. They brought their letters to nearby coffee houses and inns. They picked up their mail there, too.

**The Fastest Mail**

Mail sent between New York and Philadelphia in 1776 took about two or three days to get there. That was very fast for those times, because the roads between those cities were good.

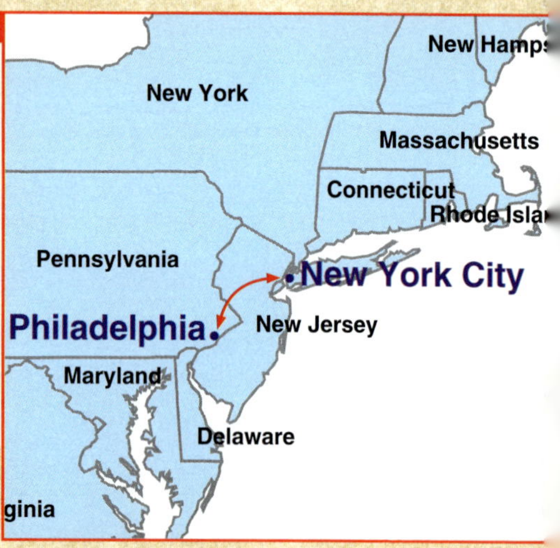
New Hamps
New York
Massachusetts
Connecticut
Rhode Isla
Pennsylvania
New York City
Philadelphia
New Jersey
Maryland
Delaware
ginia

Postriders delivered mail, but they only left when there was enough mail to pay for the trip. They rode horses or walked. There were not many good roads, so travel took many days.

The best way for mail to travel was by ship. Ships brought mail to and from people in Europe and other colonies.

It was usually fast. But people had to wait until the ships were ready to travel. Sometimes bad weather slowed them down, too.

## Ben Franklin

In 1753, Ben Franklin became the first Postmaster General in the colonies. He improved mail delivery. Even so, all the mail delivered in 1753 was less than all the mail delivered in New York City in one day today.

There was not as much paper then as there is today, and mail was expensive to send. So, people sometimes used "cross-hatching" in their letters to save money. They wrote in one direction to fill the paper, and then they turned the letter sideways and wrote across it again!

# Mail *Now*

Today there is very good mail service. People bring their mail to post offices and mailboxes.

Mail is delivered almost every day, often right to people's homes. Letters from across the country are sent fast by plane, train, and truck.

### That's Fast!
A person today can send an e-mail from the eastern United States to England in three seconds. In the 1700s, it took a ship two months of good weather to bring a letter that far.

There are modern mail inventions, too. People use their computers to send e-mail letters around the world. That is the fastest mail yet.

Some people think that telephones and cell phones are the biggest communication difference between then and now. They make communication easy just about everywhere in the world. People thousands of miles apart can seem very near to each other when talking on the phone.

People can send voice mail messages, too. They are left on telephone answering machines.

# News *Then*

## What Size?
Newspapers then were about 10 by 15 inches. Today most newspapers are about 12 by 23 inches.

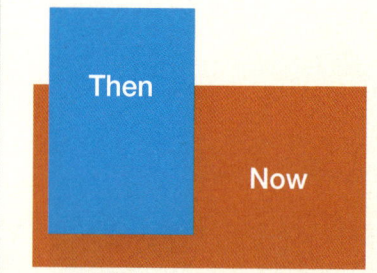

## How Many?
By the early 1800s, there were almost 600 daily newspapers. Today there are about 1,500.

Newspapers then were small, often about four pages. They were filled with poetry, advertisements, and essays, but very little news. Most were printed once each week.

Newspaper printing press from the late 1700s

### The Rags
Newspapers then were printed on paper made from rags. That may be why people sometimes call newspapers today "the rags."

Few people read them. Not many people could read well, and they were too busy anyway. Often, people just told each other the news they heard.

Newspapers then were hard to deliver. They were often sent only to people in the towns where they were printed. Many people might share one newspaper.

# News *Now*

Today newspapers have many pages. They are filled with all kinds of news. Most are printed daily.

Millions of people read them. They get their own papers delivered to their houses, or they buy them at stores and newsstands. They are easy to get. People can even get newspapers from around the world!

This graph shows the top five daily newspapers today by circulation. In the late 1700s, the top newspaper circulation was only about 1000!

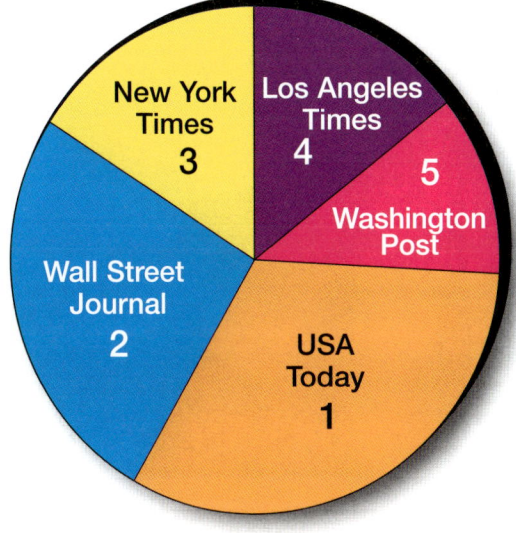

| | | |
|---|---|---|
| 1. | 2.25 million | 32% |
| 2. | 1.8 million | 26% |
| 3. | 1.1 million | 16% |
| 4. | 1.0 million | 14% |
| 5. | 0.8 million | 12% |

People today also get news in other ways. They watch television, listen to the radio, and read news on the Internet. News is everywhere!

# A Whole New Communication

There is a whole world of communication people have today that they did not have long ago. Now people have telegraphs, telephones, televisions, and more.

These three inventions begin with the word *tele*. Tele is a Greek word that means "from afar." That is what these

inventions do. They let people communicate from far away.

Today, voices and written words are sent across wires and satellites to reach around the world and even into space! People can send messages to almost anyone, anywhere, at any time.

# Communication Time Line

How has communication changed from the early days to now? Read this time line.

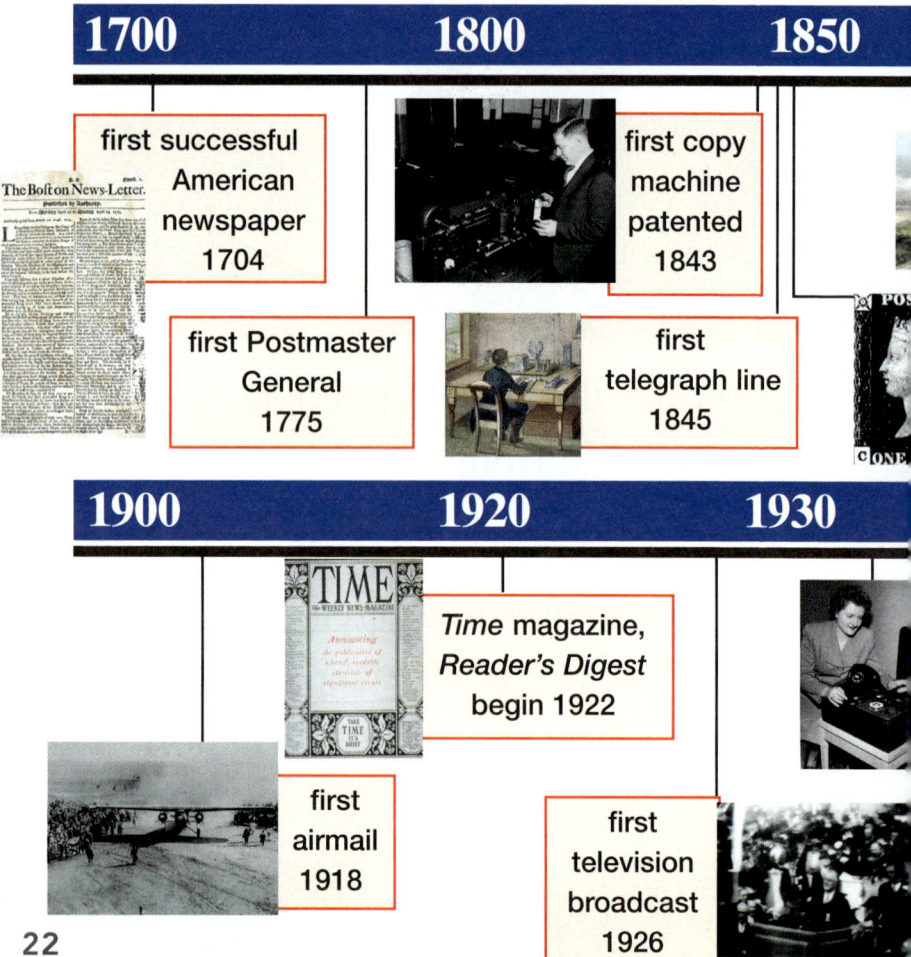

**1700**

first successful American newspaper 1704

first Postmaster General 1775

first copy machine patented 1843

first telegraph line 1845

**1800**

**1850**

**1900**

*Time* magazine, *Reader's Digest* begin 1922

first airmail 1918

first television broadcast 1926

**1920**

**1930**

## 1860 — 1875 — 1900

Pony Express begins 1860

postage stamps first used for the mail 1847

invention of the telephone 1876

first typewriter 1874

first wireless radio 1901

## 1960 — 1970 — 1975

first telephone answering machine 1935

picturephone (videophone) introduced at the World's Fair 1964

ZIP codes first used on mail 1963

first e-mail computer program created 1972

first portable cell phone 1973

23

# Glossary

**cell phone**  short for *cellular telephone*; wireless telephone that can be carried anywhere

**colonies**  the first thirteen American settlements that were ruled by England until the Revolutionary War

**communication**  the way people tell each other things

**cross-hatching**  writing on a letter in two directions that cross each other

**delivered**  sent

**e-mail**  short for *electronic mail*; messages that are sent from one computer to another through the Internet system

**fax machine**  short for *facsimile machine*; copies words and pictures and sends them through telephone lines to other facsimile machines

**Internet**  computer system that connects computers so they can communicate with each other

**newsstand**  small, open building where newspapers and magazines are sold

**Postmaster General**  the head of the postal service

**post office**  place where mail is sorted before delivery to homes and businesses

**postrider**  mail delivery person from long ago

**slang**  words people make up or use in new ways

**telegraph**  machine that sends messages through wires by using special codes

**vocabularies**  words people know without using the dictionary